Mama, Where Do Strays Go?

ROBYN L STACEY

DEDICATION

In memory of all the dogs and cats who were stray,
abandoned and/or homeless for whatever reason,
especially the little kitten found in need of medical care by
a woman who asked for help over the internet, but then,
decided to leave it to die alone instead of taking it in for
fear it might make her kids sick.

To all those who work tirelessly in animal rescue offering
their time & services to rescue, nurse and find furever
homes for as many stray, abandoned and/or homeless
animals as possible.

For Mom, who taught me to love animals from an early
age. Before it was cool, she would go to the local "pound"
to get the animals on their "last day", get their shots, nurse
them to health and find them homes.
And Dad for understanding.

Hidden from the world, in a quiet place, a
mother cat gave birth. One... two... three...
four... four little kittens. Carefully she cleaned
each and every one and nuzzled them to nurse.

Time passed quickly as the mama cared for her newborns. Soon, the little ones' eyes opened and with them an entire new world.

One evening, as Mama and her kittens settled in for the night, the littlest kitten snuggled up close and asked, "Mama? If all pets go to heaven, where do strays go?"

"Well," she started, as she pulled him a little closer, "my mama told me when a stray dies, the heavens open and an angel comes down from between the clouds. The angel gently lifts the soul of the stray, tucking him under her wings, as she soars to the heavens above. Soon, the stray is bathed in bright light, peace fills his heart and God, Himself, takes his soul, which never got a chance to shine while alive, and places it among the stars in heaven to shine for all eternity, lighting the way for many other strays trying to make it through the night."

"Wow," gasped the littlest kitten, "maybe someday, I can be a star shining so bright lighting the way."

His mama smiled, "Maybe. You never know. Now, go to sleep, my little Star."

The mama cat watched as her little ones grew. She often thought back to the evening her littlest one asked about where strays go. She didn't want her babies to be strays even if it did mean they would become stars in the night. She wanted for them what she never had: to be cared for, talked to, played with, to be warm at night and never to be lonely, but most of all, to be loved.

She thought to herself, it's time for them to go. She had to try to find them a home, a place to call their own where they will be a stray no more. She took each one in her mouth, telling the others she'd be back, and brought each one to an animal lover's home.

One... two... three... three kittens delivered safe and sound. One more left, as she once again headed back.

The littlest kitten waited his turn. He waited and waited. It seemed forever since his mama came for the third kitten. Frightened, he remembered his mama's last words, "stay put, my littlest one. I'll be back for you soon enough." But when? It was getting dark and growing colder. His little tummy rumbling with hunger. "Hurry, Mama," he quietly cried. "I'm so lonely, if only I had someone to talk to," the little kitten whispered aloud, "and maybe someone to play with."

The next day, a dragonfly swooped by. "Mr. Dragonfly?" the kitten called out.

"Yes?" he questioned back with a cock of his head.

"Can you tell me when my mama's coming back?"

"Well, I don't rightly know, littlin. She's probably just stopped to get you some food."

"I am hungry," the little kitten cried, "do you think she'll be back soon?"

"I'm sure she will," the dragonfly answered gliding out of sight.

Later, a bunny rabbit hopped by with her young
kits. The littlest kitten asked the bunny rabbit,
"Mrs. Bunny Rabbit, have you seen my mama?"

"I'm sorry, littlin, I have not. I'm sure she'll be
back soon. You can play with my youngins until
we leave," the mama bunny rabbit replied.

The little kitten and the baby bunnies played for a while as the mama bunny looked for a fresh dandelion patch.

As night fell, it grew cold. The littlest kitten shivered. He wondered aloud, "Where are you mama?"

"Don't worry, little fella," came a voice from beneath the weedy grass.

"Who are you?" the startled kitten asked pawing at the ground where the voice came from.

"Just your common ordinary black cricket," he replied.

"My mama told me to wait here for her. She's been gone an awful long time. I'm cold and lonely. I don't know when she will be coming back," the kitten explained.

"Well, I'm sure she will be along soon. In the meantime, my friends and I will stay with you tonight. We will sing you a lullaby to help you sleep!" the cricket exclaimed.

"Oh, that would be nice," the kitten answered, as he tried to keep his tired eyes open, watching for his mama.

As the littlest kitten curled into a fuzzy ball, the little black cricket gathered his friends. Altogether, the crickets began to serenade the littlest kitten with a special lullaby chirp just for him. Sleep soon came.

The morning air was gentle but warm for morning had brought the warmth of the sun. The littlest kitten basked in the sun's warm rays. Warm at last. He stretched; so, he could feel the sun's warmth all over. Along with the sun was the feeling of a gentle caress, which overcame his little body.

Believing it to be his mother, the littlest kitten picked up his tiny head and looked around. Yet, there was no one around.

He was, once again, all alone and he cried out, "Mama, you said you'd come back for me. Now, I'm alone and growing weak. I'm scared, Mama; it's getting hard to breathe."

Just as he drew a deep breath, taking in the fresh morning air, out of the shadows of some tall grass, a figure appeared...

"Mama! You did come back," the littlest kitten squealed.

"Yes," she whispered back.

"You've been gone a long time," said the kitten.

"I know. I tried to come for you but there was an accident," explained the mama.

"An accident?" he questioned as he tilted his head trying to understand.

"Yes, I was bringing your brother and sisters to their new home where people would care for them and they would no longer be strays..." her voice trailed off.

"What happened?" he asked.

"I had to cross a large road with fast cars and trucks speeding this way and that way," she said as she motioned the two different directions with her head.

"What'd you do?" he curiously questioned.

"Each time I crossed I waited; I watched.
Again and again to get each of your siblings.
The last time I crossed to come back for you..."
her voice again trailed off as she bowed her
head.

"Mama? What happened?" the kitten quietly
asked.

"I misjudged. I didn't see it. I didn't see that one car. I'm sorry I made you wait so long," she said as she raised her head and smiled at the little kitten.

"Well, it's alright, Mama. You're here now. You came for me just like you said!" the littlest kitten exclaimed.

"Yes, I did!" the mama cat stated, as she spread her angel wings, "come now, we have to go."

"Mama, you have wings," the kitten declared. "Yes," she said as she gently tucked her littlest kitten under her wings.

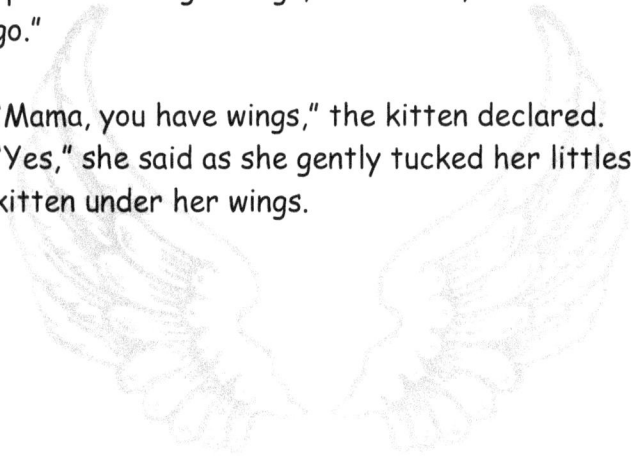

"We going to the place where the people will care for us?" he asked, distracted.

"Better," his mama answered, "a place where there's no more hunger, no more loneliness, no more cold, no more fear, no more tears."

Before he knew it, the littlest kitten and his mama were soaring towards the heavens above. The clouds separated before them.

The littlest kitten and his mama were bathed in bright light, peace filled their hearts and a voice spoke comforting the littlest stray kitten...

"Be not afraid, little one, for I made you, and although you had no one to care for you, I cared for you. When you whispered you wished for someone to talk to, I sent the dragonfly. When you needed someone to play with, I sent a mama bunny rabbit and her kits. When it was dark and you were lonely and could not sleep, I sent the crickets to serenade you to sleep. It was I who sent the warmth of the sun after such a cold night. And right before you drew your last breath, it was I who reached down from the heavens and gave you a gentle caress. When you had no one to love you, I loved you."

"Mama said God takes us strays and places them among the stars when we die..." the littlest kitten began, as his mama looked on smiling.

God smiled at the littlest kitten and his mama. Then, God, Himself, took their little souls, which never got a chance to shine while alive, and placed them among the stars in heaven to shine for all eternity, lighting the way for many other strays trying to make it through the night.

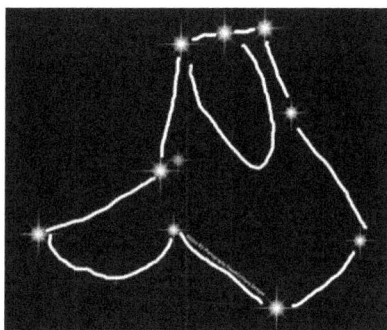

Orion the Dog
(part of Orion's Belt)

So, when you look up to the heavens tonight, if
you see a star shining real bright, think of the
littlest kitten and his mama lighting the way
for all the little strays; so, they make it
through the night alright.

This story was inspired by a little star who's light went out too soon and now lights the way for other strays.

ABOUT THE AUTHOR

Robyn Stacey is an animal caretaker/rescuer, photographer, graphic designer and writer. She inherited her love of animals from her mom and her interest in photography from her dad & maternal grandma. Her photography & Paws4Critters graphic design line can be purchased around the internet at:

robyn-stacey.pixels.com
www.robynstaceyphotos.etsy.com
www.cafepress.com/paws4critters
www.cafepress.com/americausa

She is a proud US Air Force brat and native Texan. Quotes: "My hope is for folks to see beyond the man-made world and, instead, see the beautiful world God has bestowed upon us!" and "Pawsing for Critters with Four Paws!"

You can like her on Facebook at:
www.facebook.com/robynstaceypaws4crittersphotography

www.ingramcontent.com/pod-product-compliance
Lightning Source LLC
Chambersburg PA
CBHW061201040426
42445CB00013B/1772